Mourning Love

A Poetic Journey of Love and Death

VICTORIA CRYSTAL

Order this book online at www.trafford.com/07-1140
or email orders@trafford.com

Most Trafford titles are also available at major online book retailers.

Note for Librarians: A cataloguing record for this book is available from Library and Archives Canada at www.collectionscanada.ca/amicus/index-e.html

ISBN: 978-1-4251-3112-8

We at Trafford believe that it is the responsibility of us all, as both individuals and corporations, to make choices that are environmentally and socially sound. You, in turn, are supporting this responsible conduct each time you purchase a Trafford book, or make use of our publishing services. To find out how you are helping, please visit www.trafford.com/responsiblepublishing.html

Our mission is to efficiently provide the world's finest, most comprehensive book publishing service, enabling every author to experience success. To find out how to publish your book, your way, and have it available worldwide, visit us online at www.trafford.com/10510

www.trafford.com

North America & international
toll-free: 1 888 232 4444 (USA & Canada)
phone: 250 383 6864 • fax: 250 383 6804 • email: info@trafford.com

The United Kingdom & Europe
phone: +44 (0)1865 722 113 • local rate: 0845 230 9601
facsimile: +44 (0)1865 722 868 • email: info.uk@trafford.com

10 9 8 7 6 5 4 3 2

Dedication

This book is lovingly dedicated to my husband, Henry "Vell" Crystal.

Special thanks for encouragement and inspiration:

My Heavenly Father
Tonya Presley
Dr. Doris Johnson
Tania Eastman

Introduction

On May 7, 2006, a man that I loved deeply, my husband, Henry Revell Crystal died, two days before our fourteenth anniversary. This book of poetry chronicles the emotions that we shared during his brief illness and the grief and pain that I experienced after his death. It was truly the hardest thing that I have ever endured in my life...and I still suffer tremendous bouts of grief because of his death. I had not written since my first publication of poems, *Midnight Journeys*, in 1999 and thought my poetic well had indeed run dry. When his birthday came around, I wrote my first poem in years titled, “Missing You”, and soon began to write more and more. Though cathartic, it has been a bittersweet journey. Around this time I was introduced to the music of Josh Groban and he became an integral part of my creative flow. His melancholic music calmed me, but the sad melodies helped me to keep my frame of mind as I listened to him incessantly. I cried and cried, but was determined to complete this work. So with many tears, and thanks to Josh Groban, I offer this book of poetry and pray it may help someone else who is trying to heal from losing someone that they loved so very, very dearly as I did my “Vell” as he was called. The second portion called “Roses and Thorns” deals with my husband and others who have been important in my life...the ups, downs, good and bad. The poems “Sweet Dark Love” and “Ebon Knight” shows how intensely I loved Vell and will always miss him.

THE TEAR

My love has been ill for a time..
He speaks to me of funeral clothes..
This I do not wish to hear..
Are you leaving me baby?
I have no choice ..he says..
It is not my wish..or will..
But baby..I am tired..
My love has suffered silently..
He utters no complaints..
We look at each other..
He smiles..I fight tears..
He wishes strength for me..
I cannot falter..
For my love's wish is my concern..
I go to my love and kneel..
Laying upon the lap that I love..
At his feet…I say..
I do not want you to go..
He strokes my long and silky hair..
But my love does not speak..
I look up into his face..
And there I see..a tear..

THE CONVERSATION

I sat at my love's feet,
As we viewed our blessed union,
Our joy which could not be contained,
My bridal glow...the moon would envy,
His face, so full of life and love,
Now gaunt and hollow,
Yet his eyes never veered,
We lived again the day we wed,
Once ended we look at each other,
And I say to my love,
Do you wish to tell me anything?
Except that you will leave me,
At this he says...
I have loved you from the beginning,
I hope you know this...
You have been the love of my life.

I SEE HIM

On the eve before my love dies..
He is with the man of God..
They pray and talk..
As he prepares to leave me..
To join Him…
Can one envy God?
I stroke his brow..
Lovingly… I wipe his face..
My love is slipping away..
I cannot call him back..
But the man of God is there..
Of whom he loves and reveres..
They talk of God and pray again..
The man of God is at his feet..
I…beside his bed..
My love's eyes are closed..
Yet he begins to speak..
I see Him…he says..
As I watch this wonder..
The man of God inquires..
Do you still see Him?
No…my love says..
Seconds pass..
I see Him now…
I am full and cannot speak..
This thing is too beautiful..

SATURDAY NIGHT INTO SATURDAY MORNING

It is Saturday night…
My love lays dying..
I stroke his beautiful face..
His strong but gentle hands..
I love you babe…you know that..
Yes..he says..
Hours pass and again I say..
I love you babe…you know that..
Yes…he whispers..
Sunday morning comes..
My love lays dying..
I stroke his breast..
He does not stir..
So again I say..
I love you babe..you know that..
But my love no longer speaks..
I hold him and I kiss him..
For now.. there is only..
Silence………..

SUNDAY MOURNING

O my love..speak to me..
I will not hear death's rattle..
Speak..my love..
But my love says nothing..
I hold and stroke his hand..
I speak to him of love..
Yet he does not reply..
He inhales sharply..
And my heart stands still..
Seconds pass..
My love opens his eyes..
He does not look to me..
But to his journey's end..
His stare seems far away..
He breathes again..
And I wait..
But my love breathes no more..
His raging pulse is still..
His heart..O my dear heart..
Beats no more..
My one true love…is gone.

THE FIRST NIGHT

I go into my love's room..
The smell is medicinal…sanitized..
I lay where..hours before..he lay..
So peaceful..so beautiful..
But no breath of life in him..
I hold his pillow and cry..
It has the smell of my love..
I lay..where hours before…
I watched as his soul left his body..
And I could not snatch it back..
Did you need him, Lord…
Oh God…I do..desperately..
The night is quiet…still..
By choice..I am alone…
I do not wish to share..
For perhaps his soul lingers…
Perchance…he may speak to me..
But no…still the night is silent..
I sleep..and there I dream of him..
Only to wake to his pillow and my tears..
Oh my love…come back to me..
Beautiful and whole..
I fall asleep again..
If dreams are all there are..
I will begin again..to dream.

Illustration: Lynn Downham

BLACK NIGHT

I stand alone..
The night is black and horrid...
I have just looked upon my love..
It is the last time I shall see his face..
Beauty that was life, now cold..so still..
My heart is torn, it is hollow..
Can one endure such and live..
My sons lift me and take me away..
O God, my God, are you cruel..
To take my love from me.
O beauty, where are you..
Who will now fill my arms..
This night..black..cold..
A spring night that hosts a winter's chill..
Is it not fitting..
For I am cold and dark of heart..
I stand alone, cloaked in black..
His slippers warm my feet..
Yet nothing warms my heart..
They stare at me..
They do not know...
I wish to join him,
My heart cannot endure this..
O this night..cold..black...
And here I stand..alone..
O beauty..where are you?

THE FUNERAL…PART 1

The dread of this day is upon me..
My mind is in a haze..
Oh my love..my great enduring love..
How can I let you go..
Watch as you go down…
Descend into that eternal hole..
I could crawl into a corner..
Curl up and hide..but not..
They wait for me...
Eyes..staring..questioning my state..
Oh God..why a heart of flesh..
Rather it was stone..or glass..
Then this heart could shatter..
Perhaps a shard would pierce my brain...
And I would not think or feel..
This is too hard ...too hard..
My sons walk close beside me..
I step into the church..
Looking not left or right..
But to a flag draped coffin..
Wherein is the heart of me..
Oh love...love..my soul's completion..

THE FUNERAL…PART 2

My mind is in a haze..
The process goes on..it is life..
I want to scream..but silently I cry...
And in my mind..the eternal thought..
Why..why..why..
He made no great strides in life..
But he was the heart and soul of me..
I cannot bear this pain..
Fling open the coffin..
Would my tears upon his face..
Stir him back to life..
Oh God..what shall I do now..
Without my love..my life..
Can one continue with a soul..
That has now been cut into shreds..
They sing...they speak..
They do not feel my pain..
We are at the grave..
Words spoken..not heard..
Affection shown..not wanted..
Give me nothing........
Unless it is my love..
But this farce..is life..
They say I must go now..
Not see them lay him low...
Through the window...
I stare..I cannot bear to leave him there..
Oh my love...goodbye...
Until then..our love..
To be continued..

THE GRAVE

My love is in the earth..
Unkind death has taken him..
My heart cannot bear it..
So cold ..so alone..
His beautiful eyes..wasting..
His incredible smile..wasting..
Arms that held me oh so gently..
Yet so strong..wasting..
Hands..that held..that touched my face..
Wasting.. hands that caressed my body..wasting..
Worms will take no note of him...
His immaculate clothing..
His body that joined with mine..
In perfection...
His name..carved in stone..
Speaking nothing of this man so vital..
For cruel death intruded..
Into our lives and took from me..
My love....

PRIDE

A man should go swiftly..
But death is often cruel..
Men should not suffer decline..
But go by misadventure..
Or slip away suddenly..quietly..
God has made man in His image...
And gave this image such pride..
Yet lingering death...this pride...would steal..
One should never see the eyes of a man..
In helplessness..nor shame..
Men should go swiftly..
But the heart of death is black..
The soul is not enough..It bends and breaks the spirit..
Bringing the lofty low...
A man should go swiftly..
But death is often cruel.

ANGER

My anger could destroy the earth..
Rage fills every nuance of my body..
O love..you made love to this death..
How could you leave me so..
Yet I cannot hate that which I love..
That which I miss with such an ache..
O God..he was my only love..
Could You have spared him..for me...
With You..I have anger..and fear..
For You...I do need..O God..
I am a woman..undone..in shreds..
A woman in form and visage..
Yet in heart..a shell..
My heart strings..not flesh and blood..
But bands of cold steel..of iron..
All the rivers of the world..
Cannot contain my tears..
This thing is too hard..
I am angry...at that which I loved..
He has taken my heart into the grave..

RAGE

My last tears were not shed the day they buried you,
Nor did my anger subside, that it should come to this,
Your lust for life would beckon death,
I will forever hate the mind of you that did not
fight this death,
That beast that loved you not as I,
The dark companion of night,
Who steals life's glowing light,
Even your tiny flicker,
Oh that I could have blown and it grew,
Brighter and brighter,
Binding you to our life and love,
But you covered my lips....
And stole away into darkness..
I shall forever mourn you in love..and anger.

LOVE'S LAMENT

I sleep in darkness, darkness that one may touch
Wake me not, unless my love be with you,
Unless he lay not in the earth, but between my breasts,
I feel my love, the sweetness of his loins,
His arms about me, as I die, not of want...but ecstasy,
My love calls my name, I feel his touch and I wake,
I reach out to him my fingers grasping air,
What an unkind beast is death, to take so soon, my love,
Pricked by the thorns of death...
Am I a coward, of for fear of God do I not follow,
In life, an arm's length from me, was too far from my love,
I am a year with no spring, a tree, black and barren,
Leaves fallen, trampled under deaths cold feet,
I will sleep again, there is my love,
For when I wake, there is only love of grief,
For loss of love.....
Grief, my only sustenance, take it not away...

GRIM WEEPINGS

Ah death..a cruel hound that stalks its prey..
Taking so soon love in its bud...
Oh that death had eaten a feast before you..love,
That is was fat and full..
But death is never sated..
Devouring heaping portions..
Of the hearts of those it leaves to mourn..
Cruel..cruel death..
You have killed my heart..
Sat back and with icy hands..
Wiped your mouth..laughed..
And again began the hunt..

SUMMER MOURNING

Last summer I sat and watched a film,
That did rend my heart to shreds,
All night I cried free flowing tears,
That life could be so cruel to such a love,
Knowing not that my tears were prophetic,
That I would hear such songs in my head,
Or indeed my life would play these scenes,
It was beyond thinking of even the thought,
Life sat me there last summer,
Cruelty sits me here today,
To stare at my love's unflowered grave,
For why should beauty cover,
Where beauty lies cold and still beneath.

MISSING YOU

When love is snatched from your heart
It leaves a wound that cannot be patched or mended
Time only is left to obscure the pain
My chocolate dove, you flew away from me
And what shall I do with my love for you
But to bury it deep within the recesses of that hole
Which is now in my heart
O my love, missing you is an infinite ache
Because our joy in each other was complete
As beautiful as your dazzling smile
As hypnotic as your big and sleepy eyes
Which I can no longer feel or touch
But see now only in my dreams

WHO WILL LATCH MY SANDALS?

It's the little things..my dove..
Today..I could not latch my sandals..
So I just sat there and cried..
Last week ...a dress that I could not zip..
I needed you..I remembered the kick you got ..
When you latched my shoes..
And stroked my caramel colored legs..
The blouses that buttoned at the back..
It's the little things..my dove..
Changing the light bulbs..
Strong hands that opened bottle caps..
Or jars that I struggled with..
When I dress and stand in the mirror...
You are not there to smile proudly..
Saying things like..where is my camera?
I cry sometimes because you cannot see me..
You were my greatest mirror..
I felt beauty through your eyes..
It's the little things ..my dove..
I do miss you so..

THE PICTURE

I found a picture today..
Your coat is draped around me..
Yet I do not remember this..
You tower over me..
You smile that smile..
The one you wore so well...
Like a bejeweled African king...
I would give all my earth's worth..
To see that smile again..
To feel those arms..
To fight with you..to love with you..
Such longings..so worthless..
I content myself with thoughts..
With memories and dreams..
But, oh God..I do not understand..
Help me to dull this pain..
Can this hollow ache find a name..
Any name will slight it..
So I put the picture away..
And as many nights before..I sit..I cry..
I pray to God and ask..why..why..why..

LET GO

I know..I know..
You are gone...
I saw you leave..I felt you go..
Yet I look for you..
Daily expect you to open the door..
You..not here..it is too unreal..
My mind can't wrap around it..
Those arms I miss..I seem to feel...
Your hearty laugh..I seem to hear...
And oh that smile..now eternal..
I see...even in my dreams...
You are gone..my love
But you have not let me go..
My heart is filled with you...
My memories are intense...
This hurt is just too deep..
To tear my heart from my breast..
Could not hurt me more..
My life..my whole heart..
I do miss you so..
Reaching..longing..but touching naught..
A word...a phrase..a song..
Brings you back to me..
Then..beauty..I remember..
You..my love..are gone..
My mind tells me this..
My heart hears it not..
Yet..I know..I know...I know..
You are gone..

TIME

One day at a time..they say..
Oh how many hours there are..
In one minute of the day..
And so many minutes in a second..
And each second..each minute..
Can affect a change..
In one second laughter becomes tears..
Minutes loom before you like days..
This is the depth of my loss..
Weeks pass and all the thoughts are good..
Then suddenly..despair overtakes me..
Pain..fear..panic..unspeakable grief..
I am overwhelmed..but silent..
My God..my patient God..
You suffer long with me..and my anger..
For you know my need for You..
Is greater than my rage..
But O God...why...why..I need him so..
Time..that thief..that false and cold comfort..
I needed more of you..cruel time..
But you heal..they say..
I am not yet the proof of that..
So..time..who cares not..
Or waits for none..
I wait on you..to pass..
To mend..to heal..and to free..
Free me to be again..with my heart..
My soul..my love..my love..oh love
Wait for me..my sweet..we will be..
In time................

SEASONS

When you left me..it was spring..
And as seasons change..my longing grew deeper..
The sweltering heat of summer..
Found me daily at your grave..
The sun kissing my skin..
As I grew darker outside and in...
Yet I could not stay away..
It is all that I have left..
Even knowing you were not really there..
Not my beautiful soul..
For I did see as God took that soul away..
Still..it is all that I have left..
Fall comes and my tears increase..
And with each tear..my strength..
As I look at your pebble strewn grave..
I take note of falling leaves..
Hues of yellow, red and orange..
Life ..or the semblance thereof..
Goes on..as seasons change again..
Winter comes in with a shattering ache..
It is the season of joy..but I fall into despair..
Oh my love..I miss you so..
Can one heart stand so much..
Soon..spring will come again..
It is the season that you that you flew..my dove..
Still...I will stand before your grave..
For it is all that I have left..

DOVE OF MY HEART

I pity all who know not love..
And such a one was I...
An orphan of the heart and soul..
Until God smiled ..
And sent my love to me..
Oh my dove..my chocolate dove..
You were for me..
Roses..thorns..and fears aside..
We took the ride..for life..
Perfect..you were not..
Neither..love...was I..
But we were perfect..together..
Our bond was that of love..
You poured words so sweet..
Into thirsty wounded ears..
And filled my life with love..
Our souls conjoined...to such a degree..
That death alone would part us..
My dove..my sweet souls dove..
I do think of you..long for you..
This is no time for strength..
My strength is in the grave..
For this you would surely scold me..
But oh my heart..my beloved heart..
You were my blanket of strength..
My mirror of beauty..my gracious walk..
My pride..my perpetual joy..
You..my dove..were my everything..

ALL THAT…AND MORE

When you came...I knew love...
When you came..I felt beauty..
You set me above the stars in heaven..
And gave me a name..
I felt I could not breathe ...
But by your breath..
Through your eyes..
Those eyes that adorned me with beauty..
That looked on me with such love..
From which great loves of ancient books..
Would shrink in envy..
You gave curves and form ...
To a body..flawed and scarred..
Held my face as though it was porcelain..
That would break with little pressure..
We lay down and two became one..
We were as one body..melding..
This was a wondrous thing..
Shall I know this love again..
It matters not..
For I have known love..
I have known great passion..great desire..
I knew all of this...when you came...

SOLITUDE

Where are the stars tonight..
And where is my love...
As heavens stars are beyond my grasp,
So is my love,
If I should scream and pierce the night,
With my longing for his touch,
Would this light and gentle breeze,
Bring the matter to you..
If I screamed inside my mind,
Would this lay to rest desires
You have awaken in me,
But desire, why have you cursed me so,
And love, oh love...
A star has appeared, dare I hope,
No, but it is alone,
Shall I sit under this vast canopy, hoping,
For two or three or thousands,
Oh this night, a single star...and me.

INFINITE LOVE

My soul, once released,
We meet in an open meadow,
In velvet grass and flowers of timeless beauty,
Marred not by the ages,
They neither wither, nor fade,
But change with our whims of love,
Winds whistling through eternal trees
Bid us dance,
Blithely we glide through contented lilies
With ever so light a foot,
We take our fill of love onto purposeful petals,
Our sweet souls sleep stirred by morning birds,
With this again begins our love,
That death could not constrain.....

WHERE ARE YOU?

O my love...I think of you..
You are a constant in my mind..
What now fills your days..
Do you instruct the angels..
Tell them how to dress..
In this you were perfection..
I could not miss you more...
If you were these hands..torn from me..
And I could not sorrowfully write..
O precious heart..my heart...
What will I do with the night..
But ache and yearn for you..
I pray to dream of you..
For God to grant me this..
I cannot see you..touch you..
Feel you...you are gone..
Forever...gone..unbearable sorrow..
Is my companion now..
I move through time ..
As one who is a sculpture..
Unfeeling..as eyes watch me..
To know my secret heart..
Time..that incredible thief..
Whose beauty and gifts are brief..
Yet time has no heart to feel..
No occasion to love..to miss..
But she will one day..
Bring us together again..
But now my love..I think of you.

THE PEBBLE

In front of my love's picture..
Sits a single pebble..
That I took from his grave..
I look at his beautiful smiling face..
That I loved for so few years..
And smile..then..I see the pebble..
I need the pebble there..
A harsh...unkind reminder..
That the smile has left this earth..
Only memories remain..
At times many do not understand..
A funeral does not close a door..
But opens a cold and barren one..
They do not wish to hear..
They do not wish to see..
That your life has been so horribly altered..
So you are often quiet..
About what is crushing you..
But..alone..you sit..you cry..
You stare at a beautiful man..
And...a pebble....

Illustration: Leslie McMillan

THE CLOCK

One day my love found a clock..
And placed it upon the wall..
This clock did not keep time..
From now until then..
The time stands at ten past three..
It is made of fine mahogany..
With beautiful carved designs..
Adorning its sturdy glass...
Yet it does not keep time..
My love placed this clock..
And never took it down..
Because words are written within..
These words made him hang the clock..
Though it does not keep time..
The words are these...
To have and to hold..
From this day forward..
For better..for worse
For richer, for poorer..
In sickness and in health..
To love and to cherish
Till death do us part..

THE HEARTS

Above my door..upon leaving..
Daily I see two entwined hearts..
Placed there by my love..
I thought this very strange..
For my love was very tidy..
Order and beauty was his way..
And on this thing we did contend..
But he was firm in his resolve..
The look of them is that of a child's project..
Something done ..perhaps in school..
It is brown and made of straw..
And bears the look of a mass of tangled hair..
Then...for me.. it held no beauty..
The meaning now has changed..
As now so many others..
The times you said you loved me..
And I soared..
The times you said you loved..
And I didn't feel you..
Oh love..this I do regret..
But this heart, this ragtag heart..
It was his desire to let all know..
That this was a house of love..
Two hearts..sometimes ragged..worn..
But always..always..entwined..in love.

Illustration: Lynn Downham

Roses & Thorns

THE LEVEL OF LOVE

When we first met..my love,
I had no sense of self..or worthiness..
My esteem was in a miry pit..
Beaten down ..pummeled with words...
You made beauty of me..
Through your heart..at last..
I felt love..and I did love..
Your touch..so soft..so wonderful..
Yet again..wild..as the drums of Africa..
You took me there..
In your eyes..when you lay me down..
My reflection was not the visage I kept..
In those eyes I saw a woman of beauty..
In face and form..Oh my love..
The ride was wild..the beauty...
And often...pain..so bitter ..so sweet..
But I would take that ride again..
For a thousand years with you..
These things...love..I will keep..
You..me...us...and love..
The great leveler.......

Illustration: Leslie McMillan

THE FLOWERS

It is my birthday..
And I do not wish to wake..
But a sweet aroma stirs me..
I blink away the night's sleep..
And there I see my love..kneeling..
Smiling ..a huge toothy grin..
And in his hands are flowers..
That he has liberated ...
From gardens along a path he walked..
In no particular order...
Nor was any one the same..
Such a ragged bunch...
Diamonds he has given me..
Beautiful costly pearls..
And many gifts of gold..
Yet the best...those flowers...
Were the sweetest..most precious gift..
That I have occasion to remember..

DEEP

It is a day of beauty..
Yes, it is God's day..
As my love and I ride and share..
I ask him..
Why did you marry me, love?
He speaks of my honesty and virtue..
But sees that the woman in me wants more..
That a vain thread is running crushed across my ego..
He continues...
I have not been left wanting of women..
Life owes me nothing there...
Using..being used..loving..being loved..
But you ..my babe..
Are the first..in all of this..
That I lay down...love by night..
And when the day breaks..
I am happy..to look again into your face.

RENEWED VOWS

My love..do you wish to marry me again?
Yes..my sweet replies..
It has been ten swift years..
Since the time..at first..we wed..
I cannot count my blessings..
Or voice what his love has been..
For all would think ..surely it is untrue...
And one need not boast of love..
True love is seen by all..
Roses...thorns..but love..always love..
He has esteemed me..loved me
And I have loved him...
With such great love..
That I should have another heart..
Into which my love should pour..
My love..why do you wish to marry again?
My love looks at me..his eyes so true..
So full..that he was slow to speak..
My dove..my babe..he says
Don't you know...
I am more in love with you..
Than I was the first day we wed..
I think of you while working..
When I come home...
And see your face..it is all I need..
Everything then..is fine in my world..
The day comes...
My love seems indifferent..

At which my anger rises..
But what I did not know..
My love was very ill..
And at home he did go straight to bed..
My heart again swelled with love..
For even ill..he was determined..
Again..for me to be his bride.

SWEET DARK LOVE

Sweet, black chocolate man,
You are music that moves through my soul,
Touching where no thought can reach,
Rich, smooth, sweet dark chocolate man.
I could melt and pour you over my body,
Like silk, you would cling to me.
Should I nibble you,
Therein you would last my life..
To nibble you is like standing naked before
Crashing water on stones,
It's sprinkles tease my body,
Though pleasant, it leaves me wanting.
I delight in chunks of you,
Tasting till I am full,
Sick with the sweetness of you,
Still, I crave your deliciousness,
My love, my sweet dark chocolate man...

BLISS

I am a woman of power, fearless,
A bold black queen, till my man touches me,
Towers over me, searches my soul,
He draws from me my strength,
I am a willing slave,
He is my mighty black king,
Crushed beneath his beauty,
I have no will, nor want of will,
But his pleasure,
As the sun takes the day, he takes me,
And I cry, this thing is too beautiful,
I melt into oneness with him,
His black skin blinds me with its radiance,
I kiss him, for I cannot speak,
I am bound by his deliciousness,
Tomorrow I wield my power,
Tonight my king commands.

EBON KNIGHT

My love is the beauty of blackness,
Smooth, stately, a resplendent Ethiop jewel,
Ivory of the indomitable beast line his jaw,
As stars give beauty to the night,
His touch weakens me,
The lack thereof would send me into madness,
Should he tear my heart from me,
As a wild beast does his prey,
I would beckon for the nectar of his loins,
Till my cursed desire was sated,
I lie beneath the strength of his arms,
As he tastes the sweetness of my breasts,
The budding glow of dawn steals my love from me,
Will he come again?
When the wretched hours of daylight,
Turn to beauteous darkness, as art thou,
Quickening the dull state of my heart.
I will not stir again but by your touch,
My love comes, come, my love,
Kiss me with sweet full lips,
I will drink the dark wine of his love,
For he is mine and I am ever his.

DEATH..WITH A DIFFERENCE

My love has been in the earth...
For ninety days and two..
This day I look upon a man..
His still form..speaks nothing..
Of his cold and brutal ways..
That I should have married such a man..
My mind cannot now conceive..
But for two beautiful stately sons..
Gods consoling gift...
I would have no memory of him..
Those hands..the terror of them..
Who..why was there such a man..
Did he love..did he feel..
I shall never know..
The icy hands of death has muted his tongue..
Still..I pray he reconciled with God..
This man..so different than my love..
Yet both are in the grave..
The grave..it waits..for all..

SOUL YEARINGS

Shut down the world...
Make love to me...
Dim the lights...close the door..
Do not think..do not speak..
Hold me till I hurt no more..
Smother me with hot dark kisses..
Kindle this smoldering fire...
I want no more dream lovers...
Set my body ablaze..still my mind..
Hold me in your arms...
Look into my eyes..
You look so deep..my sweet..
Fill up the darkness in my soul..
I need this...
We will not talk of love..
Love will find itself...
Shh my sweet..do not speak..
Crush me..
Love me till I have no breath..
Heart touching heart..
Soul touching soul..
I need this ..my sweet..
Right here..right now...for this moment..
Shut down the world..
And make love to me..

CLOUDED LOVE

Black clouds loom..
Your eyes..pressing against them..
Will not see love...
Betrayal smothers ones heart..
Pronounces a judgment...
And sentences love to death..
But dear heart..love will not die..
It has no fear of challenge..
Love..overcomes...and always wins..
For love is of God..
And fear...it is a vicious adversary..
Who laughs at wasted love..
Soar above the clouds ..
The darkness is no more..
There..is sunshine..love..
Laughter..and me..
My steps lead away..
But still...my heart waits..

REMEMBER ME

Darkness...beauty...pain..
the ghost who stole my soul,
the ghost who lives and breathes
immersed in history,
remember me, my love,
so cold...so sweet, inside your mystery,
your mystery..my pain..and tears fall,
shards of truth..denial..feelings..
remember me, my love,
darkness..beauty..pain..grief,
eyes.. those eyes, piercing..stealing...fleeing..
feelings denied..self wars...trepidation
and we both lose,
remember me, my love,
careful...careless..spoken words,
regrets..silence..mental islands,
discover me, love,
let love be...then you will be free,
loving, living...in chocolate dreams..
O sweet mystery, let me touch you there,
reach your island..
wake with my strength..
love with God's will...
remember me, my love.

FEAR

Take my hand..sweet one..
Do not think of fear…
God will shield us..
Love will be our canopy..
I am not deep..just woman..
A woman who loves deeply..
Take my hand..my sweet..
Time is not our friend…
She would steal us in the bud of love..
Trust God..but love me..
Life alone..unshared..is not life..
But a vague semblance thereof..
Sweet one..new love tastes of honey..
Like the kisses of your mouth..
Fear but a little..it excites love..
Still..do not let me go..
Do not forget your pain..
Bring the pain to me…
I will soothe it with the balm of love..
Sweet..take my hand..I wait..
To love again..with you..

THE DREAM

Nine months to the day that my love died..
As before..I dreamed of him...
But there was someone with him..
It was a man I knew..
This did not bother me..until..
My love left me with the man..
Smiled and disappeared..
I awoke from the dream..sobbing..
Gut wrenching..bitter tears..
My spirit was vexed for days..
Clouds of gloom covered my heart..
I did not understand..
Am I to dream no more of you..
My angel..my protector..my guide..
On this thing..I could not be consoled..
It was not about the other man..
God takes these things in hand...
But Oh love..don't leave me ..
Not again..I need you...
Dreams are all I have..
So I pray and pray and pray..
My love does not come..
So I cry and cry and cry..
Oh love, please come...
Yet my love does not come..
My food displeases me...
My sleep is disturbed..

Until...
My love comes again..
He smiles..we talk and we laugh..
And maybe for just a season..
My world is right again..

ETERNAL LOVE

When one dies..in love..
Love is then forever..
Love is a power unto itself..
For God has fashioned love...
Memories may dim..
But..my..love..you are always in my heart..
We were one soul..joined by bonds of love..
Till death..and then only did we part..
You did not desire me to be alone..
But..oh love...give me strength..
To love..to live again..
Help me not to kick at love..
To despair not..because it is not you..
This..I do not even desire..
My heart cannot endure so great a love..
To happily be stolen away..
Still..you must empty out my heart..
For it to fill again..
I wait...my love..
I wait...on you and time..

OPEN HEART

Oh this present heart...
So filled with cumbersome grief..
Yet now so open..so alone..
A heart alone will stumble..
For it cannot hold..
Cannot touch incorporeal love..
The need to love and to be loved..
Often makes one a fool..
Help me my love...
Visit me in dreams..
Guide me to love that feels like music..
Of a smooth kind..
Melodies that gently tug at my heartstrings..
Love chosen and graced by God...
Surely love..you know..you are with Him..
For then..this love would be kind..
I have no fear of love..it is life..
Life...fully realized...
My days long..my nights..endless..
Filled with tears..empty arms..
And an aching heart...
My love..speak to me in dreams..
To know of love again..I wait...

www.ingramcontent.com/pod-product-compliance
Ingram Content Group UK Ltd.
Pitfield, Milton Keynes, MK11 3LW, UK
UKHW041844190726
13854UKWH00002B/715